To

_____

Bronzie

_____

From

_____

Anne with love,

_____

Date

_____

12-4-4

_____

PRAYERS

of a Godly Woman

FOURTH EDITION

PRAYERS

of a Godly Woman

Table of Contents

Introduction

*B*eing a godly woman in today's world can be a daunting task. Never have expectations been higher, never have distractions been so plentiful, and never have demands been greater. Thankfully, God stands ready, willing, and able to help us in every facet of our lives *if* we ask Him. But it's important to remember that the best way to ask God for His wisdom and His strength is to ask Him *often*.

Sometimes, when it seems that we have too many things to do and too few hours in which to do them, we may be tempted to rush through the day with little or no time for prayer and meditation; when we do so, we suffer because of our mistaken priorities. But, when we set aside time each day for God, we open ourselves to His love, His wisdom, and His strength.

The fabric of daily life is woven together with the threads of habit, and no habit is more important than that of consistent prayer and daily devotion to our Creator. And this book is intended to help. This text contains 31 chapters, one for each day of the month. During the next 31 days, please try this experiment: read a chapter each day. If you're already committed to a daily worship time, this book will enrich that experience. If you are not, the simple act of giving God a few minutes each morning will change the direction and the quality of your life.

This text addresses topics of particular interest to you, a Christian woman living in an uncertain world. If you take the time to meditate upon these devotional readings, you will be reminded of God's love, of His Son, and of His promises. May these pages be a blessing to you, and may you, in turn, be a blessing to those whom God has seen fit to place along your path.

CHAPTER 1

The Prayers of a Godly Woman

And on the Sabbath day we went out of the city to
the riverside, where prayer was customarily made;
and we sat down and spoke to the women
who met there.

Acts 16:13 NKJV

On his second missionary journey, Paul met with a group of women who gathered for prayer at a riverside near Philippi. Among that group was Lydia, a prosperous woman who was "a worshipper of God" (Acts 16:14 NKJV). After encountering Paul and his group of missionaries, Lydia became a Christian; she then invited Paul and Silas to stay at her house, which they did. Later, when Paul "met with the brothers and encouraged them" (v. 40), Lydia's home became the first Christian church in Philippi.

On that same missionary journey, Paul started a small church in Thessalonica. A short time later, Paul wrote a letter to the new believers at Thessalonica that contained this powerful advice: "Rejoice always, pray without ceasing, in everything give thanks; for this is the will of God in Christ Jesus for you" (1 Thessalonians 5:16-18 NKJV).

When you "pray without ceasing," you invite God to become a full partner in every aspect of your life. When you consult your Creator on an hourly basis, you avail yourself of His wisdom, His strength, and His love. As Corrie ten Boom observed, "Any concern that is too small to be turned into a prayer is too small to be made into a burden."

So today, instead of turning things over in your mind, turn them over to God in prayer. Instead of worrying about your next decision, ask God to lead the way. Don't limit your prayers to meals or bedtime. Lydia proved that the prayers and deeds of a single godly woman can change the world—and you, too, have that power *if* you become a woman of constant prayer.

We are women, and my plea is,
"Let me be a woman, holy through and through,
asking for nothing but what God wants
to give me, receiving with both hands and
with all my heart whatever that is."

Elisabeth Elliot

God says we don't need to be anxious
about anything;
we just need to pray about everything.

Stormie Omartian

*Don't worry about anything, but in everything,
through prayer and petition with thanksgiving,
let your requests be made known to God.*

~

Philippians 4:6 HCSB

A Prayer for Today

Dear Lord, I will be a woman of prayer.
I will take everything to You in prayer,
and when I do, I will trust Your answers.

~

Amen

CHAPTER 2

God's Abundance

*I have come that they may have life,
and that they may have it more abundantly.*

John 10:10 NKJV

The Word of God is clear: Christ came in order that we might have life abundant and life eternal. Eternal life is the priceless possession of all who invite Christ into their hearts, but God's abundance is optional: He does not force it upon us.

When we entrust our hearts and our days to the One who created us, we experience abundance through the grace and sacrifice of His Son. But, when we turn our thoughts and direct our energies *away* from God's commandments, we inevitably forfeit the spiritual abundance that might otherwise be ours.

God's gifts are available to all, but those gifts are not guaranteed; God's gifts must be claimed by those who choose to follow Christ. As we go about our daily lives, may we accept God's promise of spiritual abundance, and may we share it with a world in desperate need of the Master's healing touch.

God is the giver, and we are the receivers.
And His richest gifts are bestowed not upon
those who do the greatest things, but upon
those who accept His abundance and His grace.

Hannah Whitall Smith

God has promised us abundance, peace,
and eternal life. These treasures are ours
for the asking; all we must do is claim them.
One of the great mysteries of life is why on
earth do so many of us wait so very long
to lay claim to God's gifts?

Marie T. Freeman

Jesus intended for us to be overwhelmed by
the blessings of regular days. He said it was
the reason he had come: "I am come that they
might have life, and that they might have it
more abundantly."

Gloria Gaither

*My cup runs over. Surely goodness and mercy
shall follow me all the days of my life;
and I will dwell in the house of the Lord forever.*

~

Psalm 23:5-6 NKJV

A Prayer for Today

Dear Lord, thank You for the joyful,
abundant life that is mine through Christ Jesus.
Guide me according to Your will, and help
me become a woman whose life is a worthy
example to others. Give me courage, Lord,
to claim the spiritual riches that You have
promised, and show me Your plan for my life,
today and forever.

Amen

CHAPTER 3

Living in an Anxious World

*Cast all your anxiety on him
because he cares for you.*
1 Peter 5:7 NIV

W e live in a world that sometimes seems to shift beneath our feet. From time to time, all of us face discouragement, adversity, or disappointment. And, throughout life, we must all endure life-changing personal losses that leave us breathless. When we do, God stands ready to protect us. Psalm 147 promises, "He heals the brokenhearted, and binds their wounds" (v. 3, NIV). When we are troubled, we must call upon God, and, in His own time and according to His own plan, He will heal us.

We live in a world that often breeds anxiety and fear. When we come face to face with tough times, we may fall prey to discouragement, doubt, or depression. But our Father in Heaven has other plans. God has promised that we may lead lives of abundance, not anxiety. In fact, His Word instructs us to "be anxious for nothing" (Philippians 4:6). But how can we put our fears to rest? By taking those fears to God and leaving them there.

As you face the challenges of everyday living, do you find yourself becoming anxious, troubled, discouraged, or fearful? If so, turn every one of your concerns over to your Heavenly Father. Are you a woman whose anxieties seem to overwhelm you at times? Take those anxieties to God. Are you troubled? Take your troubles to Him. Does your world seem to be trembling beneath your feet? Seek protection from the One who cannot be moved. The same God who created the universe will comfort you *if* you ask Him . . . so ask Him and trust Him. And then watch in amazement as your anxieties melt into the warmth of His loving hands.

So often we pray and then fret anxiously,
waiting for God to hurry up and do something.
All the while God is waiting for us to calm
down, so He can do something through us.

Corrie ten Boom

The moment anxious thoughts invade
your mind, go to the Lord in prayer.
Look first to God. Then, you will see the cause
of your anxiety in a whole new light.

Kay Arthur

*Therefore do not worry about tomorrow,
for tomorrow will worry about its own things.
Sufficient for the day is its own trouble.*

~

Matthew 6:34 NKJV

A Prayer for Today

Dear Lord, sometimes troubles and distractions
preoccupy my thoughts and trouble my soul.
When I am anxious, Father, let me turn my
prayers to You. When I am worried, give me
faith in You. Let me live courageously,
Dear God, knowing that You love me and
that You will protect me, today and forever.

~

Amen

CHAPTER 4

Cheerful Christianity

*A cheerful look brings joy to the heart,
and good news gives health to the bones.*
Proverbs 15:30 NIV

On some days, as every woman knows, it's hard to be cheerful. Sometimes, as the demands of the world increase and our energy sags, we feel less like "cheering up" and more like "tearing up." But even in our darkest hours, we can turn to God, and He will give us comfort.

Few things in life are more sad, or, for that matter, more absurd, than a grumpy Christian. Christ promises us lives of abundance and joy, but He does not force His joy upon us. We must claim His joy for ourselves, and when we do, Jesus, in turn, fills our spirits with His power and His love.

How can we receive from Christ the joy that is rightfully ours? By giving Him what is rightfully *His*: our hearts and our souls.

When we earnestly commit ourselves to the Savior of mankind, when we place Jesus at the center of our lives and trust Him as our personal Savior, He will transform us, not just for today, but for all eternity. Then we, as God's children, can share Christ's joy and His message with a world that needs both.

God is good, and heaven is forever.
And if those two facts don't cheer you up,
nothing will.

Marie T. Freeman

Christ is the secret, the source, the substance,
the center, and the circumference of
all true and lasting gladness.

Mrs. Charles E. Cowman

I am truly happy with Jesus Christ.
I couldn't live without Him.

Ruth Bell Graham

Christ can put a spring in your step and
a thrill in your heart. Optimism and
cheerfulness are products of knowing Christ.

Billy Graham

Jacob said, "For what a relief it is to see your friendly smile. It is like seeing the smile of God!"

~

Genesis 33:10 NLT

A Prayer for Today

Dear Lord, You have given me so many reasons
to celebrate. Today, let me choose an attitude
of cheerfulness. Let me be a joyful Christian,
Lord, quick to smile and slow to anger.
And, let me share Your goodness with
all whom I meet so that Your love might
shine in me and through me.

~

Amen

CHAPTER 5

Discovering Purpose and Finding Strength . . . Day by Day

Then He said to them all, "If anyone wants to come with Me, he must deny himself, take up his cross daily, and follow Me."

Luke 9:23 HCSB

*E*ven the most inspired women can, from time to time, find themselves running on empty. Why? Because the inevitable demands of daily life can drain us of our strength and rob us of the joy that is rightfully ours in Christ. Thankfully, God stands ready to renew our spirits, even on the darkest of days. God's Word is clear: When we genuinely lift our hearts and prayers to Him, He renews our strength.

Are you almost too weary to lift your head? Then bow it—in prayer. Offer your concerns and your needs to your Father in Heaven. He is always at your side, offering His love and His strength.

Your search to discover God's purpose for your life is not a destination; it is a journey that unfolds day by day. And, that's exactly how often you should seek direction from your Creator: one day at a time, each day followed by the next, without exception.

Are you seeking a renewed sense of purpose? Turn your heart toward God in prayer. Are you weak or worried? Take the time to delve deeply into God's Holy Word. Are you spiritually depleted? Call upon fellow believers to support you, and call upon Christ to renew your spirit and your life. When you do, you'll discover that the Creator of the universe stands always ready and always able to create a new sense of wonderment and joy in you.

There is an active practice of holiness as
we carry out, for the glory of God, the ordinary
duties of each day, faithfully fulfilling the
responsibilities given us. The passive practice
consists in loving acceptance of the unexpected,
be it welcome or unwelcome, remembering
that we have a wise and sovereign Lord
who works in mysterious ways and
is never taken by surprise.

Elisabeth Elliot

Jesus challenges you and me to keep our focus
daily on the cross of His will if we want
to be His disciples.

Anne Graham Lotz

Are you tired? Worn out? Burned out on religion? Come to me. Get away with me and you'll recover your life. I'll show you how to take a real rest. Walk with me and work with me . . . watch how I do it. Learn the unforced rhythms of grace. I won't lay anything heavy or ill-fitting on you. Keep company with me and you'll learn to live freely and lightly.

❧

Matthew 11:28-30 MSG

A Prayer for Today

Dear Lord, each day I need to walk with You.
Your presence provides me security and comfort.
As we walk together, Lord, may Your presence
be reflected in my life, and may
Your love dwell within my heart.

❧

Amen

CHAPTER 6

Genuine Discipleship

Be imitators of God, therefore,
as dearly loved children.
Ephesians 5:1 NIV

We can, if we choose, be passive Christians. We can sit back, secure in our own salvation, and let other believers spread the healing message of Jesus. But to do so is wrong. Instead, we are commanded to become disciples of the One who has saved us, and to do otherwise is a sin of omission with terrible consequences.

When Jesus addressed His disciples, He warned them that each one must "take up his cross daily and follow me" (Luke 9:23 NIV). Christ's message was clear: in order to follow Him, Christ's disciples must deny themselves and, instead, trust Him completely. Nothing has changed since then.

If we are to be genuine disciples of Christ, we must trust Him and place Him at the very center of our beings. Jesus never comes "next." He is always first. The wonderful paradox, of course, is that it is only by sacrificing ourselves to Him that we gain eternal salvation.

Do you seek to follow Christ? Then pick up His cross today and every day that you live. When you do, He will bless you now and forever.

When Jesus put the little child in the midst of
His disciples, He did not tell the little child to
become like His disciples; He told the disciples
to become like the little child.

Ruth Bell Graham

Discipleship usually brings us into the necessity
of choice between duty and desire.

Elisabeth Elliot

How often it occurs to me, as it must to you,
that it is far easier simply to cooperate
with God!

Beth Moore

Be filled with the Holy Spirit; join a church
where the members believe the Bible and
know the Lord; seek the fellowship of other
Christians; learn and be nourished by
God's Word and His many promises.
Conversion is not the end of your journey—
it is only the beginning.

Corrie ten Boom

*The LORD has already told you what is good,
and this is what he requires: to do what is right,
to love mercy, and to walk humbly
with your God.*

～

Micah 6:8 NLT

A Prayer for Today

Dear Lord, thank You for the gift of Your Son
Jesus, my personal Savior. Let me be a worthy
disciple of Christ, and let me be ever grateful
for His love. I offer my life to You, Lord, so that
I might live according to Your commandments
and according to Your plan. I will praise
You always as I give thanks for Your Son
and for Your everlasting love.

～

Amen

CHAPTER 7

A Faith That Makes Us Whole

*Have faith in the LORD your God
and you will be upheld.*
2 Chronicles 20:20 NIV

When a suffering woman sought healing by simply touching the hem of His garment, Jesus turned and said, "Daughter, be of good comfort; thy faith hath made thee whole" (Matthew 9:22 KJV). We, too, can be made whole when we place our faith completely and unwaveringly in the person of Jesus Christ.

Concentration camp survivor Corrie ten Boom relied on faith during her ten months of imprisonment and torture. Later, despite the fact that four of her family members had died in Nazi death camps, Corrie's faith was unshaken. She wrote, "There is no pit so deep that God's love is not deeper still." Christians take note: Genuine faith in God means faith in all circumstances, happy or sad, joyful or tragic.

If your faith is being tested to the point of breaking, know that Your Savior is near. If you reach out to Him in faith, He will give you peace and heal your broken spirit. Be content to touch even the smallest fragment of the Master's garment, and He will make you whole.

Faith in faith is pointless. Faith in a living,
active God moves mountains.

Beth Moore

God uses our most stumbling,
faltering faith-steps as the open door to
His doing for us "more than we ask or think."

Catherine Marshall

Faith does not struggle; faith lets God do it all.

Corrie ten Boom

Oh, the tranquil joy of that dear retreat,
Where the Savior bids thee rest,
With steadfast hope, and a trusting faith,
In His love secure and blest.

Fanny Crosby

For we walk by faith, not by sight.

2 Corinthians 5:7 NASB

A Prayer for Today

Dear Lord, help me to be a woman of faith.
Help me to remember that You are always near
and that You can overcome any challenge.
With Your love and Your power, Lord,
I can live courageously and faithfully
today and every day.

Amen

My Thoughts & Prayers
from This Week

My Thoughts & Prayers
for Next Week

_____

_____

_____

_____

_____

_____

_____

_____

_____

_____

_____

_____

_____

_____

_____

_____

_____

_____

_____

_____

_____

_____

CHAPTER 8

Who Rules?

You shall have no other gods before Me.
Exodus 20:3 NKJV

Who rules your heart? Is it God, or is it something else? Do you give God your firstfruits or your last? Have you given Christ your heart, your soul, your talents, your time, and your testimony, or have you given Him little more than a few hours each Sunday morning?

In the book of Exodus, God warns that we should place no gods before Him. Yet all too often, we place our Lord in second, third, or fourth place as we worship the gods of pride, greed, power, or lust. When we unwittingly place possessions or relationships above our love for the Creator, we must seek His forgiveness and repent from our sins.

Does God rule your heart? Make certain that the honest answer to this question is a resounding yes. In the life of every righteous believer, God comes first. And that's precisely the place that He deserves in your heart.

We may blunder on for years thinking
we know a great deal about Him, and then,
perhaps suddenly, we catch a sight of Him as
He is revealed in the face of Jesus Christ,
and we discover the real God.

Hannah Whitall Smith

God can see clearly no matter
how dark or foggy the night is.
Trust His Word to guide you safely home.

Lisa Whelchel

I lived with Indians who made pots out of
clay which they used for cooking. Nobody was
interested in the pot. Everybody was interested
in what was inside. The same clay taken out of
the same riverbed, always made in
the same design, nothing special about it.
Well, I'm a clay pot, and let me not forget it.
But, the excellency of the power is
of God and not us.

Elisabeth Elliot

Yet, O LORD, you are our Father.
We are the clay, you are the potter;
we are all the work of your hand.

～

Isaiah 64:8 NIV

A Prayer for Today

Dear Lord, Your love is eternal and
Your laws are everlasting. When I obey
Your commandments, I am blessed. Today,
I invite You to reign over every corner of my
heart. I will have faith in You, Father. I will
sense Your presence; I will accept Your love;
I will trust Your will; and I will praise You for
the Savior of my life: Your Son Jesus.

～

Amen

CHAPTER 9

Beyond Doubt

So He said, "Come." And when Peter had come
down out of the boat, he walked on the water to
go to Jesus. But when he saw that the wind was
boisterous, he was afraid; and beginning
to sink he cried out, saying, "Lord, save me!"
And immediately Jesus stretched out His hand and
caught him, and said to him, "O you of little faith,
why did you doubt?" And when they got
into the boat, the wind ceased.

Matthew 14:29-32 NKJV

ave you ever felt your faith in God slipping away? If so, you are not alone. Every life—including yours—is a series of successes and failures, celebrations and disappointments, joys and sorrows, hopes and doubts. Even the most faithful Christians encounter occasional bouts of fear and doubt, and so, too, will you.

Doubts come in several shapes and sizes: doubts about God, doubts about the future, and doubts about our own abilities, for starters. And what, precisely, does God's Word say in response to these doubts? The Bible is clear: when we are beset by doubts, of whatever kind, we must draw ourselves nearer to God through worship and through prayer. When we do so, God, the loving Father who has never left our sides, draws ever closer to us (James 4:8).

Will your faith be tested from time to time? Of course it will be. And will you have doubts about God's willingness to fulfill His promises? Perhaps you will. But even when you feel far removed from God, God never leaves your side, not for an instant. He is always with you, always willing to calm the storms of life. When you sincerely seek His presence—and when you genuinely seek to establish a deeper, more meaningful relationship with His Son—God is prepared to touch your heart, to calm your fears, to answer your doubts, and to restore your soul.

We are most vulnerable to the piercing winds of
doubt when we distance ourselves from
the mission and fellowship to which
Christ has called us.

Joni Eareckson Tada

Faith has no value of its own, it has value only
as it connects us with Him. It is a trick of Satan
to get us occupied with examining our faith
instead of resting in the Faithful One.

Vance Havner

Unconfessed sin in your life will cause you
to doubt.

Anne Graham Lotz

*When doubts filled my mind,
your comfort gave me renewed hope and cheer.*

~

Psalm 94:19 NLT

A Prayer for Today

Dear Lord, when I am filled with
uncertainty and doubt, give me faith.
In the dark moments of life, keep me mindful of
Your healing power and Your infinite love
so that I may live courageously and
faithfully today and every day.

~

Amen

CHAPTER 10

Trusting God's Guidance

*The LORD says, "I will guide you along
the best pathway for your life.
I will advise you and watch over you."*

Psalm 32:8 NLT

When we genuinely seek God—when we prayerfully seek His wisdom and His will—our Creator carefully leads us over the peaks and through the valleys of life. And as Christians, we can be comforted: Whether we find ourselves at the pinnacle of the mountain or the darkest depths of the valley, God is always there with us.

Psalm 37 teaches us that "The steps of the Godly are directed by God. He delights in every detail of their lives" (v. 22 NLT). In other words, God is intensely interested in each of us, and He will guide our steps *if* we serve Him obediently.

If you're unsure of your next step, lean upon God's promises and lift your prayers to Him. Remember that God is always near; remember that He is your protector and your deliverer. Open yourself to His heart, and trust Him to guide your path. When you do, your next step will be the right one.

It's a bit like river rafting with an experienced
guide. You may begin to panic when
the guide steers you straight into a steep
waterfall, especially if another course appears
much safer. Yet, after you've emerged from
the swirling depths and wiped the spray from
your eyes, you see that just beyond
the seemingly "safe" route was a series
of jagged rocks. Your guide knew
what he was doing after all.

Shirley Dobson

God will prove to you how good and acceptable
and perfect His will is when He's got His hands
on the steering wheel of your life.

Stuart & Jill Briscoe

If God is your Co-pilot . . . swap seats!

Anonymous

In all your ways acknowledge Him,
and He shall direct your paths.

~

Proverbs 3:6 NKJV

A Prayer for Today

Dear Lord, I am Your creation, and You created
me for a reason. Give me the wisdom to follow
Your direction for my life's journey according
to Your infinite wisdom and Your perfect
will. Lead me, Father, and let me trust You
completely, today and forever.

~

Amen

CHAPTER 11

Kindness in Action

Be kind to each other, tenderhearted,
forgiving one another, just as God through Christ
has forgiven you.
Ephesians 4:32 NLT

*I*n the book of Galatians, Paul's instructions are clear: "Carry each other's burdens" (6:2 NIV). When we do so, we follow in the steps of the One who willingly gave His life for us.

Christ demonstrated His love for us by willingly sacrificing His earthly life so that we might have eternal life: "But God demonstrates his own love for us in this: While we were still sinners, Christ died for us" (Romans 5:8 NIV). We, as Christ's followers, are challenged to share His love with kind words on our lips and praise in our hearts.

Just as Christ has been—and will always be—the ultimate friend to His flock, so should we be Christlike in the kindness and generosity that we show toward our families and our friends. But generosity and kindness do not stop there. Christ commands us to deal kindly with strangers and even with our enemies. This, of course, is a difficult task, but with Christ, all things are possible.

When we walk each day with Jesus—and obey the commandments found in God's Holy Word—we become worthy ambassadors for Him.

When we share the love of Christ, we share a priceless gift with the world. As His servants, we must do no less.

Our lives, we are told, are but fleeting at best,
  Like roses they fade and decay;
Then let us do good while the present is ours,
  Be useful as long as we stay.

Fanny Crosby

All kindness and good deeds,
we must keep silent. The result will be
an inner reservoir of personality power.

Catherine Marshall

Do all the good you can. By all the means
you can. In all the ways you can.
In all the places you can. At all the times
you can. To all the people you can.
As long as ever you can.

John Wesley

Kind words are like honey—
sweet to the soul and healthy for the body.

~

Proverbs 16:24 NLT

A Prayer for Today

Dear Lord, help me see the needs of those
around me. Today, let me spread kind words
of thanksgiving and celebration in honor
of Your Son. Let forgiveness rule my heart,
and let my love for Christ be reflected through
the acts of kindness that I extend to those
who need the healing touch
of the Master's hand.

~

Amen

CHAPTER 12

Sensing God's Presence

I am not alone, because the Father is with me.
John 16:32 KJV

*S*ince God is everywhere, we are free to sense His presence whenever we take the time to quiet our souls and turn our prayers to Him. But sometimes, amid the incessant demands of everyday life, we turn our thoughts far from God; when we do, we suffer.

Do you set aside quiet moments each day to offer praise to your Creator? As a woman who has received the gift of God's grace, you most certainly should. Silence is a gift that you give to yourself and to God. During these moments of stillness, you will often sense the infinite love and power of your Creator—and He, in turn, will speak directly to your heart.

The familiar words of Psalm 46:10 remind us to "Be still, and know that I am God." When we do so, we encounter the awesome presence of our loving Heavenly Father, and we are comforted in the knowledge that God is not just near. He is here.

If you want to hear God's voice clearly and you are uncertain, then remain in His presence until He changes that uncertainty. Often, much can happen during this waiting for the Lord. Sometimes, He changes pride into humility, doubt into faith and peace.

Corrie ten Boom

Make the least of all that goes and the most of all that comes. Don't regret what is past. Cherish what you have. Look forward to all that is to come. And most important of all, rely moment by moment on Jesus Christ.

Gigi Graham Tchividjian

Only a love that has no regard for vessels and jars—appearances or image—only a love that will lavish its most treasured essence on the feet of Jesus can produce the kind of fragrance that draws cynics and believers alike into His presence.

Gloria Gaither

The eyes of the LORD are in every place,
keeping watch . . . .

~

Proverbs 15:3 NKJV

A Prayer for Today

Heavenly Father, help me to feel Your presence
in every situation and every circumstance.
You are with me, Lord, in times of celebration
and in times of sorrow. You are with me when
I am strong and when I am weak. You never
leave my side even when it seems to me that
You are far away. Today and every day, God,
let me feel You and acknowledge
Your presence so that others, too,
might know You through me.

~

Amen

CHAPTER 13

God's Gift of Grace

My grace is sufficient for you,
for my power is made perfect in weakness.

2 Corinthians 12:9 NIV

*J*esus is the spiritual sun that gives warmth, light, and life to the world. Christ died on the cross so that we might have eternal life. This gift, freely given from God's only Son, is the priceless possession of everyone who accepts Him as Lord and Savior.

Thankfully, God's grace is not an earthly reward for righteous behavior; it is, instead, a blessed spiritual gift. When we accept Christ into our hearts, we are saved by His grace. The familiar words from the book of Ephesians make God's promise perfectly clear: "For it is by grace you have been saved, through faith—and this not from yourselves, it is the gift of God—not by works, so that no one can boast" (2:8-9 NIV).

God's grace is the ultimate gift, and we owe Him our eternal gratitude. Our Heavenly Father is waiting patiently for each of us to accept His Son and receive His grace. Let us accept that gift today so that we might enjoy God's presence now and throughout all eternity.

Grace calls you to get up, throw off your blanket
of helplessness, and to move on through
life in faith.

Kay Arthur

God does amazing works through prayers that
seek to extend His grace to others.

Shirley Dobson

How beautiful it is to learn that grace
isn't fragile, and that in the family of God
we can fail and not be a failure.

Gloria Gaither

Kindness in this world will do much to help
others, not only to come into the light,
but also to grow in grace day by day.

Fanny Crosby

*For it is by grace you have been saved,
through faith—and this not from yourselves,
it is the gift of God—not by works,
so that no one can boast.*

~

Ephesians 2:8-9 NIV

A Prayer for Today

Lord, Your grace is a gift that cannot be earned.
It is a gift that was given freely when I accepted
Your Son as my personal Savior. Freely have
I received Your gifts, Father. Let me freely share
my gifts, my possessions, my time, my energy,
and my faith. And let my words, my thoughts,
my prayers, and my deeds bring honor to
You and to Your Son, now and forever.

~

Amen

CHAPTER 14

Hope Without Wavering

*Let us hold on to the confession of our hope
without wavering, for He who promised is faithful.*
Hebrews 10:23 HCSB

As every woman knows, hope is a perishable commodity. Despite God's promises, despite Christ's love, and despite our countless blessings, we are fallible human beings who can still lose hope from time to time. When we do, we need the encouragement of Christian friends, the life-changing power of prayer, and the healing truth of God's Holy Word.

As grateful servants of Christ, we should seek to cultivate our hopes each day through quiet meditation, through devotion to God, and through association with fellow believers. But sometimes, amid the hustle and bustle of everyday living, we leave our hopes to fend for themselves, and when we do, bad things begin to happen. If we find ourselves falling into the spiritual traps of worry and discouragement, we should seek the healing touch of Jesus *and* the encouraging words of fellow believers.

This world can be a place of trials and tribulations, yet we need never lose hope. God has promised us peace, joy, and eternal life—and God *always* keeps His promises. Always.

Never yield to gloomy anticipation.
Place your hope and confidence in God.
He has no record of failure.

Mrs. Charles E. Cowman

No other religion, no other philosophy promises
new bodies, hearts, and minds.
Only in the Gospel of Christ do hurting people
find such incredible hope.

Joni Eareckson Tada

Love is the seed of all hope. It is the enticement
to trust, to risk, to try, and to go on.

Gloria Gaither

You can look forward with hope, because
one day there will be no more separation,
no more scars, and no more suffering in
My Father's House.
It's the home of your dreams!

Anne Graham Lotz

This hope we have as an anchor of the soul,
a hope both sure and steadfast.

~

Hebrews 6:19 NASB

A Prayer for Today

Dear Lord, make me a woman of hope.
If I become discouraged, let me turn to You.
If I grow weary, let me seek strength in You.
When I face adversity, let me seek Your will and
trust Your Word. In every aspect of my life,
I will trust You, Father, so that my heart
will be filled with faith and hope,
this day and forever.

~

Amen

My Thoughts & Prayers
from This Week

My Thoughts & Prayers
for Next Week

CHAPTER 15

This Is the Day!

This is the day which the LORD has made;
let us rejoice and be glad in it.

Psalm 118:24 NASB

The familiar words of Psalm 118:24 remind us of a profound yet simple truth: God created this day, and it's up to each of us to rejoice and to be grateful.

For Christian believers, every day begins and ends with God and His Son. Christ came to this earth to give us abundant life and eternal salvation. We give thanks to our Maker when we treasure each day and use it to the fullest.

This day is a gift from God. How will you use it? Will you celebrate God's gifts and obey His commandments? Will you share words of encouragement and hope with all who cross your path? Will you share the Good News of the risen Christ? Will you trust in the Father and praise His glorious handiwork? The answer to these questions will determine, to a surprising extent, the direction and the quality of your day.

So whatever this day holds for you, begin it and end it with God as your partner and Christ as your Savior. And throughout the day, give thanks to the One who created you and saved you. God's love for you is infinite. Accept it joyously and be thankful.

If you're a thinking Christian,
you will be a joyful Christian.

Marie T. Freeman

Joy is available to all who seek His riches.
The key to joy is found in the person
of Jesus Christ and in His will.

Kay Arthur

God knows everything. He can manage
everything, and He loves us. Surely this
is enough for a fullness of joy that
is beyond words.

Hannah Whitall Smith

Among the most joyful people I have known
have been some who seem to have had
no human reason for joy. The sweet fragrance of
Christ has shown through their lives.

Elisabeth Elliot

*May the God of hope fill you with all joy
and peace as you trust in him, so that you
may overflow with hope by the power
of the Holy Spirit.*

~

Romans 15:13 NIV

A Prayer for Today

Dear Lord, You have given me so many
blessings; let me celebrate Your gifts.
Make me thankful, loving, responsible,
and wise. I praise You, Father, for the gift of
Your Son and for the priceless gift of salvation.
Make me be a joyful Christian, a worthy
example to others, and a dutiful servant
to You this day and forever.

~

Amen

CHAPTER 16

Quiet Time

In quietness and confidence shall be your strength.
Isaiah 30:15 NKJV

*I*n the first chapter of Mark, we read that in the darkness of the early morning hours, Jesus went to a solitary place and prayed. So, too, should we. But sometimes, finding quiet moments of solitude is difficult indeed.

We live in a noisy world, a world filled with distractions, frustrations, and complications. But if we allow the distractions of a clamorous world to separate us from God's peace, we do ourselves a profound disservice.

If we seek to maintain righteous minds and compassionate hearts, we must take time each day for prayer and for meditation. We must make ourselves still in the presence of our Creator. We must quiet our minds and our hearts so that we can sense God's will, God's love, and God's Son.

Are you one of those busy women who rushes through the day with scarcely a single moment for quiet contemplation and prayer? If so, it's time to reorder your priorities. Nothing is more important than the time you spend with your Savior. So be still and claim the inner peace that is your spiritual birthright: the peace of Jesus Christ. It is offered freely; it has been paid for in full; it is yours for the asking. So ask. And then share.

The manifold rewards of a serious, consistent
prayer life demonstrate clearly that time
with our Lord should be our first priority.

Shirley Dobson

The more complicated life becomes,
the more we need to quiet our souls before God.

Elisabeth Elliot

In the center of a hurricane there is absolute
quiet and peace. There is no safer place
than in the center of the will of God.

Corrie ten Boom

How motivating it has been for me to view
my early morning devotions as a time of retreat
alone with Jesus, Who desires that I
"come with Him by myself to a quiet place"
in order to pray, read His Word, listen for
His voice, and be renewed in my spirit.

Anne Graham Lotz

Be still, and know that I am God.

~

Psalm 46:10 KJV

A Prayer for Today

Lord, Your Holy Word is a light unto the world;
let me study it, trust it, and share it with all
who cross my path. Let me discover You,
Father, in the quiet moments of the day.
And, in all that I say and do, help me to be
a worthy witness as I share the Good News of
Your perfect Son and Your perfect Word.

~

Amen

CHAPTER 17

Simplicity

*We brought nothing into the world,
so we can take nothing out. But, if we have food
and clothes, we will be satisfied with that.*

1 Timothy 6:7-8 NCV

*J*s yours a life of moderation or accumulation? Are you more interested in the possessions you can acquire or in the person you can become? The answers to these questions will determine the direction of your day and, in time, the direction of your life.

Ours is a highly complicated society, a place where people and corporations vie for your attention, for your time, and for your dollars. Don't let them succeed in complicating your life! Keep your eyes focused instead upon God.

If your material possessions are somehow distancing you from God, discard them. If your outside interests leave you too little time for your family or your Creator, slow down the merry-go-round, or better yet, get off the merry-go-round completely. Remember: God wants your full attention, and He wants it today, so don't let anybody or anything get in His way.

I do beg of you to recognize the extreme
simplicity of faith; it is nothing more nor less
than just believing God when He says He either
has done something for us, or will do it;
and then trusting Him to do it. It is so simple
that it is hard to explain.

Hannah Whitall Smith

It's sobering to contemplate how much time,
effort, sacrifice, compromise, and attention
we give to acquiring and increasing our supply
of something that is totally insignificant
in eternity.

Anne Graham Lotz

It is part of Satan's program to make our faith
complicated and involved. Now and then,
we need a rediscovery of the simplicity that
is in Christ and in our faith in Him.

Vance Havner

Better a little with the fear of the LORD
than great wealth with turmoil.

~

Proverbs 15:16 NIV

A Prayer for Today

Slow me down, Lord, so that I might feel Your
presence and Your peace. When the demands
of the day begin to press down upon me, let me
turn to You for strength. When I am hurried,
angered, embittered, or discouraged, keep me
mindful of Your blessings, Your commandments,
Your mercy, and Your Son.

~

Amen

CHAPTER 18

Discovering His Peace

Encourage each other. Live in harmony and peace.
Then the God of love and peace will be with you.

2 Corinthians 13:11 NLT

*T*he beautiful words of John 14:27 give us hope: "Peace I leave with you, my peace I give unto you . . . ." Jesus offers us peace, not as the world gives, but as He alone gives. We, as believers, can accept His peace or ignore it.

When we accept the peace of Jesus Christ into our hearts, our lives are transformed. And then, because we possess the gift of peace, we can share that gift with fellow Christians, family members, friends, and associates. If, on the other hand, we choose to ignore the gift of peace—for whatever reason—we cannot share what we do not possess.

As every woman knows, peace can be a scarce commodity in a demanding, 21st-century world. How, then, can we find the peace that we so desperately desire? By turning our days and our lives over to God. Elisabeth Elliot writes, "If my life is surrendered to God, all is well. Let me not grab it back, as though it were in peril in His hand but would be safer in mine!" May we give our lives, our hopes, and our prayers to the Lord, and, by doing so, accept His will *and* His peace.

God's peace is like a river, not a pond. In other words, a sense of health and well-being, both of which are expressions of the Hebrew shalom, can permeate our homes even when we're in white-water rapids.

Beth Moore

Let's please God by actively seeking, through prayer, "peaceful and quiet lives" for ourselves, our spouses, our children and grandchildren, our friends, and our nation (1 Timothy 2:1-3 NIV).

Shirley Dobson

Some hearts need a pace-maker; all hearts need the Peace-maker.

Quips, Anonymous

Jesus did not promise to change the circumstances around us. He promised great peace and pure joy to those who would learn to believe that God actually controls all things.

Corrie ten Boom

*But now in Christ Jesus you who once were
far off have been brought near by
the blood of Christ.
For He Himself is our peace.*

∼

Ephesians 2:13-14 NKJV

A Prayer for Today

Dear Lord, let me accept the peace and
abundance that You offer through Your Son
Jesus. You are the Giver of all things good,
Father, and You give me peace when I draw
close to You. Help me to trust Your will,
to follow Your commands, and to accept
Your peace, today and forever.

∼

Amen

CHAPTER 19

Optimistic Christianity

*I can do everything through him
that gives me strength.*
Philippians 4:13 NIV

essimism and Christianity don't mix. Why? Because Christians have every reason to be optimistic about life here on earth *and* life eternal. Mrs. Charles E. Cowman advised, "Never yield to gloomy anticipation. Place your hope and confidence in God. He has no record of failure."

Sometimes, despite our trust in God, we may fall into the spiritual traps of worry, frustration, anxiety, or sheer exhaustion, and our hearts become heavy. What's needed is plenty of rest, a large dose of perspective, and God's healing touch, but not necessarily in that order.

Today, make this promise to yourself and keep it: vow to be a hope-filled Christian. Think optimistically about your life, your profession, and your future. Trust your hopes, not your fears. Take time to celebrate God's glorious creation. And then, when you've filled your heart with hope and gladness, share your optimism with others. They'll be better for it, and so will you. But not necessarily in that order.

If you can't tell whether your glass is half-empty
of half-full, you don't need another glass;
what you need is better eyesight . . .
and a more thankful heart.

Marie T. Freeman

Christ can put a spring in your step and
a thrill in your heart. Optimism and
cheerfulness are products of knowing Christ.

Billy Graham

I could go through this day oblivious to
the miracles all around me,
or I could tune in and "enjoy."

Gloria Gaither

But if we look forward to something
we don't have yet,
we must wait patiently and confidently.

~

Romans 8:25 NLT

A Prayer for Today

Lord, give me faith, optimism, and hope.
Let me expect the best from You, and let me
look for the best in others. Let me trust You,
Lord, to direct my life. And, let me be
Your faithful, hopeful, optimistic servant
every day that I live.

~

Amen

CHAPTER 20

The Best Time to Praise Him

Is anyone happy? Let him sing songs of praise.
James 5:13 NIV

When is the best time to praise God? In church? Before dinner is served? When we tuck little children into bed? None of the above. The best time to praise God is all day, every day, to the greatest extent we can, with thanksgiving in our hearts, and with a song on our lips.

Too many of us, even well-intentioned believers, tend to "compartmentalize" our waking hours into a few familiar categories: work, rest, play, family time, and worship. To do so is a mistake. Worship and praise should be woven into the fabric of everything we do; it should never be relegated to a weekly three-hour visit to church on Sunday morning.

Theologian Wayne Oates once admitted, "Many of my prayers are made with my eyes open. You see, it seems I'm always praying about something, and it's not always convenient—or safe—to close my eyes." Dr. Oates understood that God always hears our prayers and that the relative position of our eyelids is of no concern to Him.

Today, find a little more time to lift your concerns to God in prayer, and praise Him for all that He has done. Whether your eyes are open or closed, He's listening.

I am to praise God for all things, regardless of where they seem to originate. Doing this is the key to receiving the blessings of God. Praise will wash away my resentments.

Catherine Marshall

Most of the verses written about praise in God's Word were voiced by people faced with crushing heartaches, injustice, treachery, slander, and scores of other difficult situations.

Joni Eareckson Tada

Two wings are necessary to lift our souls toward God: prayer and praise. Prayer asks. Praise accepts the answer.

Mrs. Charles E. Cowman

From the rising of the sun to its setting,
the name of the LORD is to be praised.

~

Psalm 113:3 NASB

A Prayer for Today

Dear Lord, today and every day I will praise
You. I will come to You with hope in my heart
and words of gratitude on my lips.
Let me follow in the footsteps of Your Son,
and let my thoughts, my prayers, my words,
and my deeds praise You now and forever.

~

Amen

CHAPTER 21

Protected by the Shepherd

The LORD is my shepherd; I shall not want.
He maketh me to lie down in green pastures:
he leadeth me beside the still waters. He restoreth
my soul: he leadeth me in the paths of righteousness
for his name's sake. Yea, though I walk through the
valley of the shadow of death, I will fear no evil:
for thou art with me; thy rod and thy staff they
comfort me. Thou preparest a table before me in the
presence of mine enemies: thou anointest my head
with oil; my cup runneth over. Surely goodness and
mercy shall follow me all the days of my life:
and I will dwell in the house of the LORD for ever.

Psalm 23 KJV

*I*n the 23rd Psalm, David teaches us that God is like a watchful shepherd caring for His flock. No wonder these verses have provided comfort and hope for generations of believers.

You are precious in the eyes of God. You are His priceless creation, made in His image, and protected by Him. God watches over every step you make and every breath you take, so you need never be afraid. But sometimes, fear has a way of slipping into the minds and hearts of even the most devout believers—and you are no exception.

As a busy woman, you know from firsthand experience that life is not always easy. But as a recipient of God's grace, you also know that you are protected by a loving Heavenly Father.

On occasion, you will confront circumstances that trouble you to the very core of your soul. When you are afraid, trust in God. When you are worried, turn your concerns over to Him. When you are anxious, be still and listen for the quiet assurance of God's promises. And then, place your life in His hands. He is your shepherd today and throughout eternity. Trust the Shepherd.

In God's faithfulness lies eternal security.

Corrie ten Boom

The center of God's will is our only safety.

Betsie ten Boom

The Lord God of heaven and earth,
the Almighty Creator of all things, He who
holds the universe in His hand as though it
were a very little thing, He is your Shepherd,
and He has charged Himself with the care and
keeping of you, as a shepherd is charged with
the care and keeping of his sheep.

Hannah Whitall Smith

When we get to a place where it can't be done
unless God does it, God will do it!

Vance Havner

O righteous God, who searches minds and hearts,
bring to an end the violence of the wicked
and make the righteous secure.

~

Psalm 7:9 NIV

A Prayer for Today

Dear Lord, You protect me; help me to learn
how to protect myself. Help me to slow down,
to think ahead, and to look before I leap.
You are concerned with my security, Lord.
Help me to be concerned with it, too.

~

Amen

My Thoughts & Prayers
from This Week

My Thoughts & Prayers
for Next Week

CHAPTER 22

Beginning the Day with God

It is good to give thanks to the LORD,
to sing praises to the Most High.
It is good to proclaim your unfailing love
in the morning, your faithfulness in the evening.

Psalm 92:1-2 NLT

*E*ach new day is a gift from God, and if we are wise, we spend a few quiet moments each morning thanking the Giver. We human beings are, indeed, creatures of habit, and no habit is more important to our spiritual health than the discipline of daily prayer and devotion to the Creator.

When we begin each day with heads bowed and hearts lifted, we remind ourselves of God's love, His protection, and His commandments. And if we are wise, we align our priorities for the coming day with the teachings and commandments that God has given us through His Holy Word.

Are you seeking to change some aspect of your life? Do you seek to improve the condition of your spiritual or physical health? If so, ask for God's help and ask for it many times each day . . . starting with your morning devotional.

We all need to make time for God.
Even Jesus made time to be alone
with the Father.

Kay Arthur

Morning praise will make your days.

Quips, Anonymous

What digestion is to the body,
meditation is to the soul.

Warren Wiersbe

A life lived without reflection can be
very superficial and empty.

Elisabeth Elliot

*Morning by morning he wakens me and
opens my understanding to his will.
The Sovereign LORD has spoke to me,
and I have listened.*

~

Isaiah 50:4-5 NLT

A Prayer for Today

Heavenly Father, in these quiet moments
before this busy day unfolds, I come to You.
May my meditations bring You pleasure
just as surely as they bring me a clearer sense of
Your love and Your peace. May the time
I spend in quiet meditation mold my day
and my life . . . for You.

~

Amen

CHAPTER 23

Pleasing People

Versus

Pleasing God

Our only goal is to please God whether we live here or there, because we must all stand before Christ to be judged.

2 Corinthians 5:9-10 NCV

When God made you, He equipped you with an array of talents and abilities that are uniquely yours. It's up to you to discover those talents and to use them, but sometimes the world will encourage you to do otherwise. At times, society will attempt to cubbyhole you, to standardize you, and to make you fit into a particular, preformed mold. Perhaps God has other plans.

Sometimes, because you're an imperfect human being, you may become so wrapped up in meeting *society's* expectations that you fail to focus on *God's* expectations. To do so is a mistake of major proportions—don't make it. Instead, seek God's guidance as you focus your energies on becoming the best "you" that you can possibly be. And, when it comes to matters of conscience, seek approval not from your peers, but from your Creator.

Whom will you try to please today: God or man? Your primary obligation is not to please imperfect men and women. Your obligation is to strive diligently to meet the expectations of an all-knowing and perfect God. Trust Him always. Love Him always. Praise Him always. And seek to please Him. Always.

It is comfortable to know that we are
responsible to God and not to man.
It is a small matter to be judged
of man's judgement.

Lottie Moon

Being loved by Him whose opinion matters
most gives us the security to risk loving,
too—even loving ourselves.

Gloria Gaither

As you and I lay up for ourselves living, lasting
treasures in Heaven, we come to the awesome
conclusion that we ourselves are His treasure!

Anne Graham Lotz

When we are set free from the bondage of
pleasing others, when we are free from currying
others' favor and others' approval—then no one
will be able to make us miserable or dissatisfied.
And then, if we know we have pleased God,
contentment will be our consolation.

Kay Arthur

Obviously, I'm not trying to be a people pleaser!
No, I am trying to please God. If I were still
trying to please people,
I would not be Christ's servant.

~

Galatians 1:10 NLT

A Prayer for Today

Dear Lord, today I will honor You with
my thoughts, my actions, and my prayers.
I will seek to please You, and I will strive to
serve You. Your blessings are as limitless as
Your love. And because I have been so
richly blessed, I will worship You, Father,
with thanksgiving in my heart and
praise on my lips, this day and forever.

~

Amen

CHAPTER 24

Beyond Fear

*Don't be afraid, because I am your God.
I will make you strong and will help you;
I will support you with my right hand
that saves you.*

Isaiah 41:10 NCV

*E*ven the most dedicated Christian woman may find her courage tested by the inevitable disappointments and tragedies of life. After all, we live in a world filled with uncertainty, hardship, sickness, and danger. Old Man Trouble, it seems, is never too far from the front door.

When we focus upon our fears and our doubts, we may find many reasons to lie awake at night and fret about the uncertainties of the coming day. A better strategy, of course, is to focus not upon our fears, but instead upon our God.

God is as near as your next breath, and He is in control. He offers salvation to all His children, including you. God is your shield and your strength; you are His forever. So don't focus your thoughts upon the fears of the day. Instead, trust God's plan and His eternal love for you. And remember: whatever the size of your challenge, God is bigger.

God shields us from most of the things we fear,
but when He chooses not to shield us,
He unfailingly allots grace in
the measure needed.

Elisabeth Elliot

Worry is a cycle of inefficient thoughts
whirling around a center of fear.

Corrie ten Boom

If a person fears God, he or she has no reason to
fear anything else. On the other hand,
if a person does not fear God,
then fear becomes a way of life.

Beth Moore

One of the main missions of God is to free us
from the debilitating bonds of fear and anxiety.
God's heart is broken when He sees us so
demoralized and weighed down by fear.

Bill Hybels

Don't be afraid, because the Lord your God will be with you everywhere you go.

~

Joshua 1:9 NCV

A Prayer for Today

Dear Lord, when I am fearful, keep me mindful that You are my protector and my salvation. Thank You, Father, for a perfect love that casts out fear. Because of You, I can live courageously and faithfully this day and every day.

~

Amen

CHAPTER 25

The Search for Wisdom

Those who are wise will shine like the brightness of the heavens, and those who lead many to righteousness, like the stars for ever and ever.

Daniel 12:3 NIV

*T*he fruit of wisdom is found in the garden of God's Holy Word. If we call upon our Lord, if we study His teachings, and if we seek to see the world through His eyes, He gives us guidance, wisdom and perspective. When we make God's priorities our priorities, He leads us according to His plan and according to His commandments. When we study God's Word, we are reminded that *God's* reality is *the ultimate* reality. But sometimes, when the demands of the day threaten to overwhelm us, we lose perspective, and we forfeit the blessings that God bestows upon those who accept His wisdom and His peace.

Do you seek to live according to God's plan? If so, you must study His Word. You must seek out worthy teachers and listen carefully to their advice. You must associate, day in and day out, with godly men and women. And then, as you accumulate wisdom, you must not keep it for yourself; you must, instead, share it with others. But be forewarned: if you sincerely seek to share your hard-earned wisdom with the world, your actions must give credence to your words. The best way to share one's wisdom—perhaps the only way—is not by proclamation, but by example.

Are you a woman who embraces God's wisdom? And do you apply that wisdom to every aspect of your life? If so, you will be blessed by Him . . . today, tomorrow, and forever.

Knowledge can be found in books or in school.
Wisdom, on the other hand,
starts with God . . . and ends there.

Marie T. Freeman

This is my song through endless ages:
Jesus led me all the way.

Fanny Crosby

Wisdom is knowledge applied. Head knowledge
is useless on the battlefield. Knowledge stamped
on the heart makes one wise.

Beth Moore

If any of you lacks wisdom, he should ask God,
who gives generously to all without finding fault,
and it will be given to him.

~

James 1:5 NIV

A Prayer for Today

Lord, make me a woman of wisdom and
discernment. I seek wisdom, Lord, not as
the world gives, but as You give. Lead me in
Your ways and teach me from Your Word so
that, in time, my wisdom might glorify
Your kingdom and Your Son.

~

Amen

CHAPTER 26

The Journey Toward Spiritual Maturity

*Long for the pure milk of the word,
so that by it you may grow in respect to salvation.*
1 Peter 2:2 NASB

he journey toward spiritual maturity lasts a lifetime: As Christians, we can and should continue to grow in the love and the knowledge of our Savior as long as we live. When we cease to grow, either emotionally or spiritually, we do ourselves and our loved ones a profound disservice. But, if we study God's Word, if we obey His commandments, and if we live in the center of His will, we will not be "stagnant" believers; we will, instead, be growing Christians . . . and that's exactly what God wants for our lives.

Many of life's most important lessons are painful to learn. But spiritual growth need not take place only in times of adversity. We must seek to grow in our faith every day that we live.

In those quiet moments when we open our hearts to God, the One who made us keeps remaking us. He gives us direction, perspective, wisdom, and courage. And, the appropriate moment to accept those spiritual gifts is the present one.

We had plenty of challenges, some of which were tremendously serious, yet God has enabled us to walk, crawl, limp, or leap—whatever way we could progress—toward wholeness.

Beth Moore

Recently I've been learning that life comes down to this: God is in everything. Regardless of what difficulties I am experiencing at the moment, or what things aren't as I would like them to be, I look at the circumstances and say, "Lord, what are you trying to teach me?"

Catherine Marshall

I'm not what I want to be.
I'm not what I'm going to be.
But, thank God, I'm not what I was!

Gloria Gaither

I do not know how the Spirit of Christ performs it, but He brings us choices through which we constantly change, fresh and new, into His likeness.

Joni Eareckson Tada

Grow in grace and understanding of our Master and Savior, Jesus Christ. Glory to the Master, now and forever! Yes!

~

2 Peter 3:18 MSG

A Prayer for Today

Lord, help me to keep growing spiritually *and* emotionally. Let me live according to Your Word, and let me grow in my faith every day that I live.

~

Amen

CHAPTER 27

Sharing the Good News

But when the Holy Spirit has come upon you,
you will receive power and will tell people about me
everywhere—in Jerusalem, throughout Judea,
in Samaria, and to the ends of the earth.

Acts 1:8 NLT

One way that we demonstrate our love for others is by sharing the Good News of Jesus Christ. The story of Jesus should be shouted from the rooftops by believers the world over. But all too often, it is not. For a variety of reasons, too many Christians keep their beliefs to themselves, and when they do, the world suffers because of their failure to speak up.

Paul offered a message to believers of every generation when he wrote, "God has not given us a spirit of timidity" (2 Timothy 1:7 NASB). Paul's meaning is straightforward: When sharing our testimonies, we must be courageous, forthright, and unashamed. As believers in Christ, we know how He has touched our hearts and changed our lives. Now is the time to share our personal testimonies with others.

The old familiar hymn begins, "What a friend we have in Jesus . . . ." No truer words were ever penned. Jesus is the sovereign friend and ultimate savior of mankind. Christ showed enduring love for us by willingly sacrificing His own life so that we might have eternal life. Let us love Him, praise Him, and share His message of salvation with our neighbors and with the world.

Your light is the truth of the Gospel message
itself as well as your witness as to
Who Jesus is and what He has done for you.
Don't hide it.

Anne Graham Lotz

God has ordained that others may see
the reality of His presence by the illumination
our lives shed forth.

Beth Moore

Choose Jesus Christ! Deny yourself,
take up the Cross, and follow Him—
for the world must be shown.
The world must see, in us, a discernible,
visible, startling difference.

Elisabeth Elliot

You are the light of the world.

Matthew 5:14 NIV

A Prayer for Today

Dear Lord, the life that I live and the words
that I speak bear testimony to my faith.
Make me a faithful servant of Your Son,
and let my testimony be worthy of You.
Let my words be sure and true, Lord,
and let my actions point others to You.

Amen

CHAPTER 28

Integrity

But also for this very reason,
giving all diligence, add to your faith virtue,
to virtue knowledge.

2 Peter 1:5 NKJV

Wise women understand that integrity is a crucial building block in the foundation of a well-lived life. Integrity is built slowly over a lifetime. It is the sum of every right decision, every honest word, every noble thought, and every heartfelt prayer. It is forged on the anvil of honorable work and polished by the twin virtues of generosity and humility. Integrity is a precious thing—difficult to build, but easy to tear down; godly women value it and protect it at all costs.

As believers in Christ, we must seek to live each day with discipline, honesty, and faith. When we do, at least two things happen: integrity becomes a habit, and God blesses us because of our obedience to Him.

Living a life of integrity isn't always the easiest way, but it is always the right way. And God clearly intends that it should be *our* way, too.

God never called us to naïveté.
He called us to integrity . . . .
The biblical concept of integrity emphasizes
mature innocence not childlike ignorance.

Beth Moore

Virtue is lovely, not merely obligatory;
a celestial mistress,
not a categorical imperative.

C. S. Lewis

Virtue is nothing but well-directed love.

St. Augustine

Lying covers a multitude of sins—temporarily.

D. L. Moody

*Finally, brethren, whatever things are true,
whatever things are noble, whatever things
are just, whatever things are pure, whatever
things are lovely, whatever things are of
good report, if there is any virtue and if there is
anything praiseworthy—
meditate on these things.*

Philippians 4:8 NKJV

A Prayer for Today

Dear Lord, You command Your children
to behave honorably. Let me follow Your
commandment. Give me the courage to speak
honestly and to walk righteously with You
so that others might see Your eternal truth
reflected in my words and my deeds.

Amen

My Thoughts & Prayers
from This Week

My Thoughts & Prayers
for Next Week

_____

_____

_____

_____

_____

_____

_____

_____

_____

_____

_____

_____

_____

_____

_____

_____

_____

_____

_____

_____

_____

_____

_____

CHAPTER 29

A Woman Who Fears the Lord

Charm is deceptive, and beauty is fleeting;
but a woman who fears the LORD is to be praised.
Give her the reward she has earned....

Proverbs 31:30-31 NIV

*A*re you a woman who possesses a healthy, fearful respect for God's power? Hopefully so. After all, God's Word teaches that the fear of the Lord is the beginning of knowledge (Proverbs 1:7).

When we fear the Creator—and when we honor Him by obeying His commandments—we receive God's approval and His blessings. But, when we ignore Him or disobey His commandments, we invite disastrous consequences.

God's hand shapes the universe, and it shapes our lives. God maintains absolute sovereignty over His creation, and His power is beyond comprehension. As believers, we must cultivate a sincere respect for God's awesome power. The fear of the Lord is, indeed, the beginning of knowledge. So today, as you face the realities of everyday life, remember this: until you acquire a healthy, respectful fear of God's power, your education is incomplete, and so is your faith.

Our God is the sovereign Creator of
the universe! He loves us as His own children
and has provided every good thing we have;
He is worthy of our praise every moment.

Shirley Dobson

There is something incredibly comforting
about knowing that the Creator
is in control of your life.

Lisa Whelchel

Most women have a sense of their spiritual side,
even those who have no professed religion or
organized affiliation with a belief system.
They have a recognition that there is a way of
life that works and that it's wrapped up
in the spiritual.

Stormie Omartian

The fear of God is the death of every other fear.

C. H. Spurgeon

She is clothed with strength and dignity,
and she laughs with no fear of the future.
When she speaks, her words are wise,
and kindness is the rule when
she gives instructions.

~

Proverbs 31:25-26 NLT

A Prayer for Today

Dear Lord, others have expectations of me,
and I have hopes and desires for my life.
Lord, bring all other expectations in line with
Your plans for me. May my only fear be that of
displeasing the One who created me.
May I obey Your commandments and seek
Your will this day and every day.

~

Amen

CHAPTER 30

Comforting Those in Need

Blessed be the God and Father of our Lord Jesus Christ, the father of mercies and God of all comfort, who comforts us in all our tribulation, that we may be able to comfort those who are in any trouble, with the comfort with which we ourselves are comforted by God.

2 Corinthians 1: 3-4 NKJV

We live in a world that is, on occasion, a frightening place. Sometimes, we sustain life-altering losses that are so profound and so tragic that it seems we could never recover. But, with God's help and with the help of encouraging family members and friends, we *can* recover.

In times of need, God's Word is clear: as believers, we must offer comfort to those in need by sharing not only our courage but also our faith. As the renowned revivalist Vance Havner observed, "No journey is complete that does not lead through some dark valleys. We can properly comfort others only with the comfort wherewith we ourselves have been comforted of God."

In times of adversity, we are wise to remember the words of Jesus who, when He walked on the waters, reassured His disciples, saying, "Take courage! It is I. Don't be afraid" (Matthew 14: 27 NIV). Then, with Christ on His throne—and with trusted friends and loving family members at our sides—we can face our fears with courage and with faith.

When we Christians are too busy to care
for each other, we're simply too busy
for our own good . . . and for God's.

Marie T. Freeman

A little kindly advice is better than
a great deal of scolding.

Fanny Crosby

When action-oriented compassion is absent,
it's a tell-tale sign that
something's spiritually amiss.

Bill Hybels

When you launch an act of kindness out
into the crosswinds of life,
it will blow kindness back to you.

Dennis Swanberg

So, as those who have been chosen of God, holy and beloved, put on a heart of compassion, kindness, humility, gentleness and patience.

Colossians 3:12 NASB

A Prayer for Today

Dear Lord, when I am troubled, You comfort me. When I am discouraged, You lift me up. Whatever my circumstances, Lord, I will trust Your plan for my life. And, when my family and friends are troubled, I will remind them of Your love, Your wisdom, and Your grace.

Amen

CHAPTER 31

Christ's Love

For I am convinced that neither death, nor life,
nor angels, nor principalities, nor things present,
nor things to come, nor powers, nor height,
nor depth, nor any other created thing,
will be able to separate us from the love of God,
which is in Christ Jesus our Lord.

Romans 8:38-39 NASB

*H*ow much does Christ love us? More than we, as mere mortals, can comprehend. His love is perfect and steadfast. Even though we are fallible and wayward, the Good Shepherd cares for us still. Even though we have fallen far short of the Father's commandments, Christ loves us with a power and depth that are beyond our understanding. The sacrifice that Jesus made upon the cross was made for each of us, and His love endures to the edge of eternity and beyond.

Christ's love changes everything. When you accept His gift of grace, you are transformed, not only for today, but also for all eternity. If you haven't already done so, accept Jesus Christ as your Savior. He's waiting patiently for you to invite Him into your heart. Please don't make Him wait a single minute longer.

There was One, who for "us sinners and
our salvation," left the glories of heaven and
sojourned upon this earth in weariness and woe,
amid those who hated him and
finally took his life.

Lottie Moon

Behold, behold the wondrous love,
that ever flows from God above
through Christ His only Son, Who gave
His precious blood our souls to save.

Fanny Crosby

So Jesus came, stripping himself of everything
as he came—omnipotence, omniscience,
omnipresence—everything except love.
"He emptied himself" (Philippians 2:7),
emptied himself of everything except love.
Love—his only protection, his only weapon,
his only method.

E. Stanley Jones

I am the good shepherd.
The good shepherd lays down his life for the sheep.

~

John 10:11 NIV

A Prayer for Today

Dear Jesus, I am humbled by Your love and
mercy. You went to Calvary so that I might
have eternal life. Thank You, Jesus,
for Your priceless gift, and for Your love.
You loved me first, Lord, and I will return
Your love today and forever.

~

Amen

My Thoughts & Prayers
for the Month

My Thoughts & Prayers
for the Month

Bible Verses to Consider

Love

*Though I speak with the tongues of men
and of angels, but have not love,
I have become sounding brass or a clanging cymbal.*

1 Corinthians 13:1 NKJV

*Beloved, if God so loved us,
we also ought to love one another.*

1 John 4:11 NKJV

*No man hath seen God at any time.
If we love one another, God dwelleth in us . . . .*

1 John 4:12 KJV

*And the Lord make you to increase
and abound in love one toward another,
and toward all men.*

1 Thessalonians 3:12 KJV

But now abide faith, hope, love,

these three;

but the greatest of these is

love.

~

1 Corinthians 13:13 NASB

Hope

Hope deferred makes the heart sick.

Proverbs 13:12 NKJV

*This hope we have as an anchor of the soul,
a hope both sure and steadfast.*

Hebrews 6:19 NASB

I find rest in God; only he gives me hope.

Psalm 62:5 NCV

*Let us hold fast the confession of our hope
without wavering,
for He who promised is faithful.*

Hebrews 10:23 NKJV

Rejoice in hope;

be patient in affliction;

be persistent in prayer.

~

Romans 12:12 HCSB

Service

*Whoever serves me must follow me.
Then my servant will be with me everywhere I am.
My Father will honor anyone who serves me.*

John 12:26 NCV

*So prepare your minds for service
and have self-control.*

1 Peter 1:13 NCV

*Shepherd God's flock, for whom you are
responsible. Watch over them because you want to,
not because you are forced. That is how God wants
it. Do it because you are happy to serve.*

1 Peter 5:2 NCV

*Jesus sat down and called the twelve apostles
to him. He said, "Whoever wants to be
the most important must be last of all
and servant of all."*

Mark 9:35 NCV

The greatest among you must
be a servant. But those who exalt
themselves will be humbled,
and those who humble themselves
will be exalted.

~

Matthew 23:11-12 NLT

Kindness

Be kind to one another, tender-hearted,
forgiving each other, just as God in Christ
also has forgiven you.

Ephesians 4:32 NASB

Be kindly affectionate to one another with brotherly
love, in honor giving preference to one another;
not lagging in diligence, fervent in spirit, serving
the Lord; rejoicing in hope, patient in tribulation,
continuing steadfastly in prayer.

Romans 12:10-12 NKJV

Here is a simple, rule-of-thumb for behavior:
Ask yourself what you want people to do for you,
then grab the initiative and do it for them. Add up
God's Law and Prophets and this is what you get.

Matthew 7:12 MSG

Assuredly, I say to you, inasmuch as you did it to
one of the least of these My brethren,
you did it to Me.

Matthew 25:40 NKJV

Carry each other's burdens,
and in this way you will
fulfill the law of Christ.

~

Galatians 6:2 NIV

Joy

*Until now you have not asked for anything
in my name. Ask and you will receive,
so that your joy will be the fullest possible joy.*

John 16:24 NCV

*Be cheerful no matter what; pray all the time;
thank God no matter what happens. This is the way
God wants you who belong to Christ Jesus to live.*

1 Thessalonians 5:16-18 MSG

*Let the hearts of those who seek the LORD rejoice.
Look to the LORD and his strength;
seek his face always.*

1 Chronicles 16:10-11 NIV

*Make a joyful noise unto the LORD, all ye lands.
Serve the LORD with gladness:
come before his presence with singing.*

Psalm 100:1-2 KJV

This is the day which
the LORD has made;
let us rejoice and be glad in it.

Psalm 118:24 NASB